DUET RECITAL

Selected and Arranged by DENES AGAY

Contents

THREE FOLK TUNES
1. Paper Of Pins

Arranged by
DENES AGAY

SECONDO

Folk Tune, U.S.A.

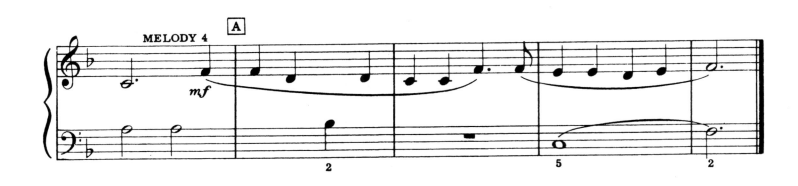

2. Alouette

Canadian Folk Song

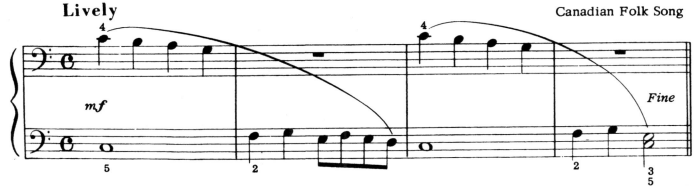

THREE FOLK TUNES

1. Paper Of Pins

PRIMO

Arranged by
DENES AGAY

Folk Tune, U.S.A.

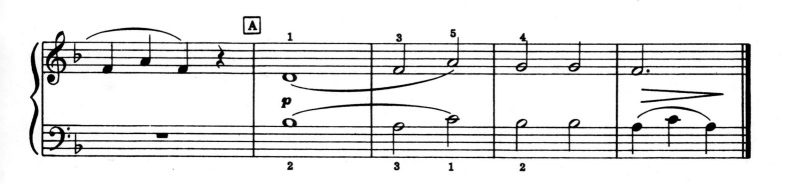

2. Alouette

Lively

Canadian Folk Song

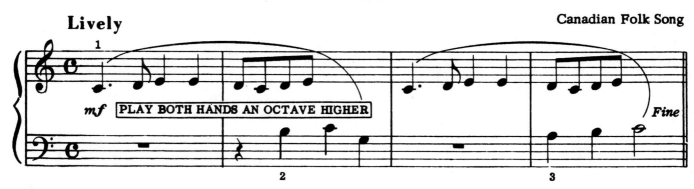

TM21816-30

3. Down In The Valley

Arranged by
DENES AGAY

Moderately slow   SECONDO

Folk Tune, U.S.A.

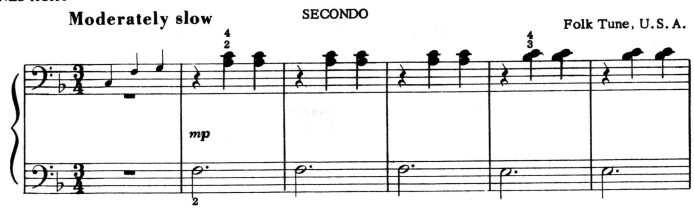

TM21816-30

3. Down In The Valley

Arranged by
DENES AGAY

PRIMO

Folk Tune, U.S.A.

Moderately slow

PLAY BOTH HANDS AN OCTAVE HIGHER

TM21816-30

TWO LITTLE PIECES
1. Cradle Song

Arranged by
DENES AGAY

SECONDO

DMITRI KABALEVSKY

Rather slow

2. Polka

Lively

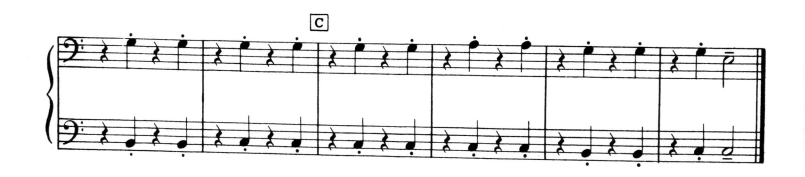

TM21816-30

TWO LITTLE PIECES

1. Cradle Song

PRIMO

Arranged by
DENES AGAY

DMITRI KABALEVSKY

2. Polka

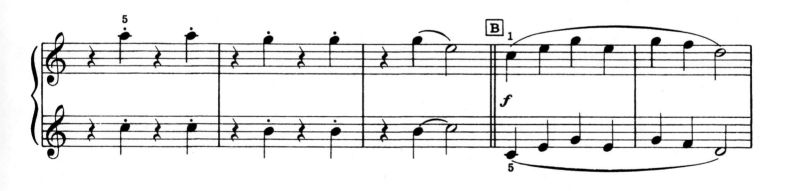

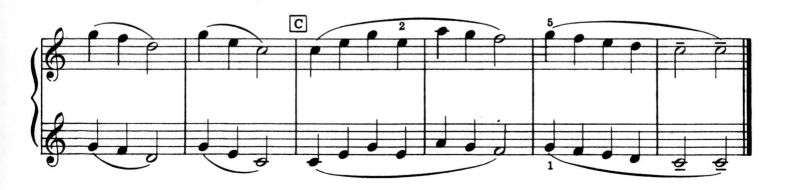

TM21816-30

THE HAPPY FARMER

Arranged by
DENES AGAY

SECONDO

ROBERT SCHUMANN

THE HAPPY FARMER

Arranged by
DENES AGAY

PRIMO

ROBERT SCHUMANN

Bright and gay

MEXICAN HAND CLAPPING SONG

(Chiapanecas)

Arranged by
DENES AGAY

SECONDO

Traditional

Lively, with marked rhythm

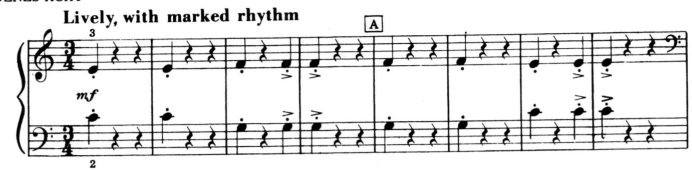

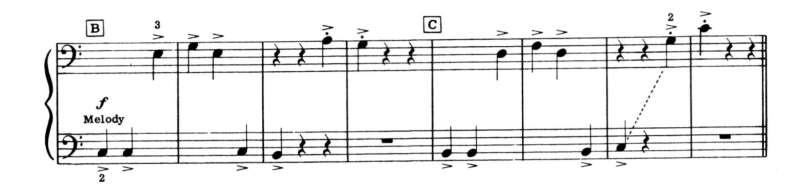

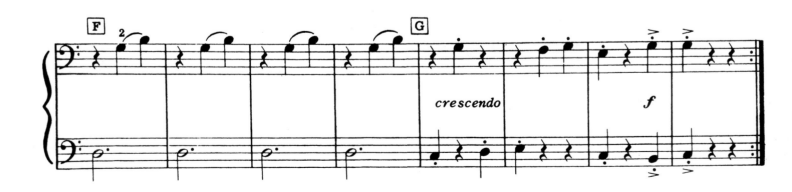

TM21816-30

MEXICAN HAND CLAPPING SONG

(Chiapanecas)

Arranged by
DENES AGAY

PRIMO

Traditional

Lively, with marked rhythm

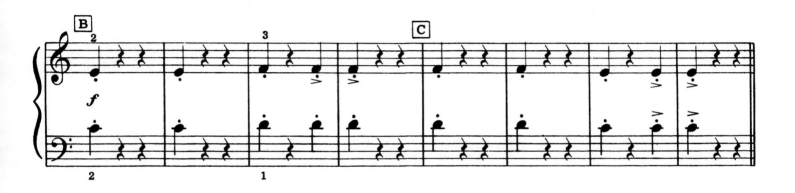

mf PLAY BOTH HANDS AN OCTAVE HIGHER

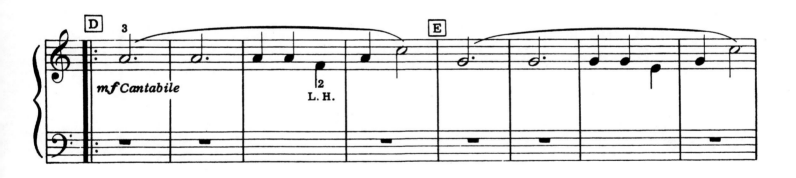

f

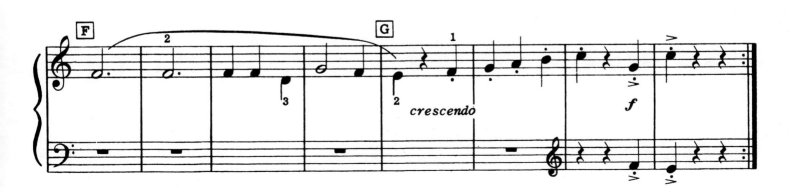

mf Cantabile
L. H.

crescendo
f

TM21816-30

Too-ra-loo-ra-loo-ral

THAT'S AN IRISH LULLABY

Arranged by
DENES AGAY

SECONDO

J. R. SHANNON

Slowly and gently

Too-ra-loo-ra-loo-ral

THAT'S AN IRISH LULLABY

Arranged by
DENES AGAY

PRIMO

J. R. SHANNON

Slowly and gently

RONDO A CAPRICCIO

(Rage Over A Lost Penny)

Arranged by
DENES AGAY

SECONDO

LUDWIG VAN BEETHOVEN

RONDO A CAPRICCIO
(Rage Over A Lost Penny)

PRIMO

Arranged by
DENES AGAY

LUDWIG VAN BEETHOVEN

TM 21816-30

THE BAGPIPERS' PARADE
(Theme from the "London" Symphony)

Arranged by
DENES AGAY

SECONDO

JOSEPH HAYDN

THE BAGPIPERS' PARADE

(Theme from the "London" Symphony)

Arranged by
DENES AGAY

JOSEPH HAYDN

PRIMO

COUNTRY GARDENS

SECONDO

Arranged by
DENES AGAY

English Folk Dance

COUNTRY GARDENS
PRIMO

Arranged by
DENES AGAY

English Folk Dance

THE THUNDERER
SECONDO

Arranged by
DENES AGAY

JOHN PHILIP SOUSA

Lively March tempo

THE THUNDERER

PRIMO

Arranged by
DENES AGAY

JOHN PHILIP SOUSA

Lively March tempo

TM21816-30

TWO HUNGARIAN FOLK TUNES

Arranged by
DENES AGAY **Moderately slow**

1.

BÉLA BARTÓK

TWO HUNGARIAN FOLK TUNES

Arranged by
DENES AGAY

1.

PRIMO

BÉLA BARTÓK

THE 'SLEEPING BEAUTY' WALTZ

Arranged by
DENES AGAY

SECONDO

PETER I. TCHAIKOVSKY

THE "SLEEPING BEAUTY' WALTZ

Arranged by
DENES AGAY

PRIMO

PETER I. TCHAIKOVSKY

MARCH

Arranged by
DENES AGAY

DMITRI SHOSTAKOVICH

SECONDO

MARCH
PRIMO

Arranged by
DENES AGAY

DMITRI SHOSTAKOVICH

SONG OF THE BELLS

From "The Magic Flute"
SECONDO

Arranged by
DENES AGAY

Lively

WOLFGANG AMADEUS MOZART

SONG OF THE BELLS

From "The Magic Flute"

PRIMO

Arranged by
DENES AGAY

WOLFGANG AMADEUS MOZART

TM 21816-30

HAVING FUN!

Arranged by
DENES AGAY

SECONDO (Teacher)

SAMUEL MAYKAPAR

HAVING FUN!

Arranged by
DENES AGAY

PRIMO (Student)

SAMUEL MAYKAPAR

Moderately fast

TM21816-30

The Young Pianist's Library
Edited by Denes Agay

The Young Pianist's Library is a complete, integrated system of piano-teaching materials providing teacher and student with a stimulating repertoire of graded teaching pieces in a variety of styles and categories to enhance any teaching approach.

SOLO BOOKS

Each solo book in *The Young Pianist's Library* is available in three graded volumes. Included are collections of original masterpieces, classical literature, folk songs, popular arrangements, and styles from Baroque to jazz.

Elementary (Level 1)
The Young Pianist's First Book (DA0001)

Late Elementary (Level 2)
From Bach to Bartók (DA0002)
Sonatinas (DA0005A)
Broadway Classics (DA0008)
Popular Recital Pieces (DA0011)
Folk Songs and Folk Dances (DA0014)
Solo Pieces of Today (DA0020)
Dances Baroque to Jazz (DA0038)
Gershwin Recital Pieces (DA0041)

Early Intermediate (Level 3)
From Bach to Bartók (DA0003)
Sonatinas (DA0006)
Popular Recital Pieces (DA0012)
Solo Pieces of Today (DA0021)

Intermediate (Level 4)
From Bach to Bartók (DA0004)
Sonatinas (DA0007A)
Broadway Classics (DA0010)
Solo Pieces of Today (DA0022)
Broadway Showcase of Famous Melodies (DA0028)
Fun with Sight Reading (DA0031)
Dances: Baroque to Jazz (DA0040)
Gershwin Recital Pieces (DA0042)
Gershwin Recital Pieces (DA0043)

DUET BOOKS

Each duet book in *The Young Pianist's Library* is available in three graded volumes and offers valuable ensemble experience in a variety of styles.

Late Elementary (Level 2)
Duet Recital Book (DA0017)
Broadway Classics (DA0032)

Early Intermediate (Level 3)
Duet Recital Book (DA0018)

Intermediate (Level 4)
Duet Recital Book (DA0019)
Broadway Classics (DA0034)

TECHNIC BOOKS

Each technic book in *The Young Pianist's Library* provides piano students with graded studies and etudes for the development of technic, style, and musicianship.

Late Elementary (Level 2)
The Technic Treasury (DA0023A)

Early Intermediate (Level 3)
The Technic Treasury (DA0024)

ISBN-10: 0-7692-3439-9
ISBN-13: 978-0-7692-3439-7

Alfred
alfred.com

DA0017

DA0017
YOUNG PIANIST'S
LIBRARY 6A: DUET
$10.95

104980
Long & McQuade